WITHDRAWN
Damaged, Obsolete, or Surplus
Jackson County Library Services

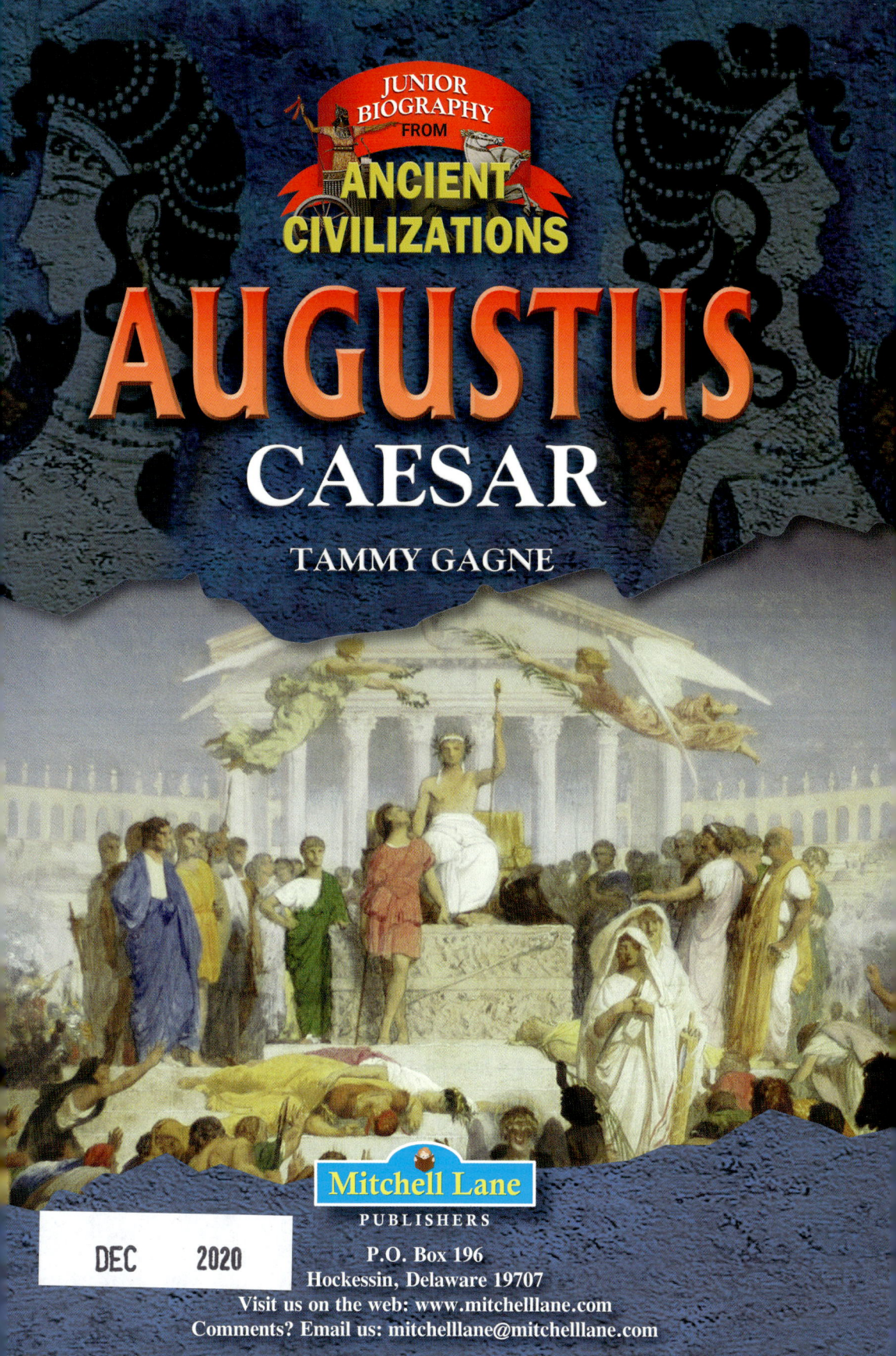

JUNIOR BIOGRAPHY FROM ANCIENT CIVILIZATIONS

AUGUSTUS CAESAR

TAMMY GAGNE

Mitchell Lane
PUBLISHERS

P.O. Box 196
Hockessin, Delaware 19707
Visit us on the web: www.mitchelllane.com
Comments? Email us: mitchelllane@mitchelllane.com

JUNIOR BIOGRAPHY FROM ANCIENT CIVILIZATIONS

Alexander the Great • Archimedes
Augustus Caesar • Confucius • Genghis Khan
Homer • Leif Erikson • Marco Polo
Nero • Socrates

Copyright © 2014 by Mitchell Lane Publishers

All rights reserved. No part of this book may be reproduced without written permission from the publisher. Printed and bound in the United States of America.

ABOUT THE AUTHOR: Tammy Gagne is the author of numerous books for adults and children, including *A Kid's Guide to the Voting Process*, *Life on the Reservations* and *Homer* for Mitchell Lane Publishers. She resides in northern New England with her husband and son. One of her favorite pastimes is visiting schools to speak to kids about the writing process.

PUBLISHER'S NOTE: The facts on which the story in this book is based have been thoroughly researched. Documentation of such research can be found on pages 44–45. While every possible effort has been made to ensure accuracy, the publisher will not assume liability for damages caused by inaccuracies in the data, and makes no warranty on the accuracy of the information contained herein.

Printing 1 2 3 4 5 6 7 8 9

Library of Congress Cataloging-in-Publication Data

Gagne, Tammy.
　Augustus Caesar / by Tammy Gagne.
　　pages cm. — (Junior biography from ancient civilizations)
　Includes bibliographical references and index.
　ISBN 978-1-61228-438-5 (library bound)
 1. Augustus, Emperor of Rome, 63 B.C.–14 A.D.—Juvenile literature. 2. Rome—History—Augustus, 30 B.C.–14 A.D.—Juvenile literature. 3. Emperors—Rome—Biography—Juvenile literature. I. Title.
 DG279.G15 2013
 937'.07092—dc23
　[B]
　　　　　　　　　　　　　　2013012551

eBook ISBN: 9781612285009

PLB

CONTENTS

Chapter One
The Battle of Actium 5
The Quinquereme 9

Chapter Two
The Boy Known as Octavius 11
Learning Opportunities 15

Chapter Three
Proving His Worth 17
The Assassination of Julius Caesar 21

Chapter Four
Caesar's Will 23
Remembering the Romans 27

Chapter Five
The "Roman Peace" 29
The Mausoleum of Augustus 39

Chronology 40
Timeline 42
Chapter Notes 43
Further Reading 44
    Works Consulted 44
    On the Internet 45
Phonetic Pronunciations 46
Glossary 47
Index 48

Phonetic pronunciations of words in **bold** can be found on page 46.

The Augustus of Prima Porta is one of the most famous images of the ruler. On display at the Vatican Museum, the marble statue shows the powerful leader addressing his army.

CHAPTER 1
The Battle of Actium

A mighty battle was fought in the Mediterranean for control of the Roman Empire in 31 BCE. On one side of this civil war was **Octavian**,* who would later become known as Augustus Caesar. He had been named the ruler of Rome more than a decade earlier after his uncle, Julius Caesar, was assassinated. Octavian's opponent, Mark Antony, believed that he deserved this title—and the power that went with it—instead.

Antony wasn't going to give up easily. He had already spent years trying to come between Octavian and the people of Rome. At times he had worked against Octavian openly. At other times he pretended to be his ally. Finally the situation came to a head. Both sides had assembled large armies and naval fleets. They met near the town of **Actium**, which was located on the western coast of Greece.

Antony had a powerful ally. Several years earlier he had fallen in love with **Cleopatra**, the queen of Egypt. She had much to gain from her relationship with Antony. If he defeated Octavian, Cleopatra would become the joint ruler of the

*For pronunciations of words in **bold**, see page 46.

CHAPTER 1

Roman Empire. She brought 60 ships to join Antony's fleet. Together their ships were both more numerous and more powerful than Octavian's.

But Octavian had a brilliant general named **Marcus Agrippa** on his side. While Antony was moving his ships into the waters near Actium, Agrippa attacked Messenia on the southwest tip of Greece. The attack came as a surprise and was a success. Agrippa continued defeating Antony's forces as he moved farther and farther along the coast.

Soon Octavian held control of both the land and the sea. He had blocked his enemy's lines of communication, as well as his access to food and other supplies. Already weak from hunger, many of Antony's men were now falling ill. Antony had more sailors than Octavian, but they were not as experienced. More importantly, Cleopatra was having second thoughts. She was carrying all of her treasure—and a great deal of Egypt's—on her ships. She wanted Antony to leave the battle and return to Egypt with her.

Antony hoped that he would be able to withdraw with his fleet. But he waited too long to make his decision. On September 2, a fight broke out that Antony could not escape.

Both fleets were divided into three wings: left, center, and right. **Lucius Policola** was the commander of Antony's right wing. When Octavian's left wing advanced toward Policola, he responded by moving outward to defend his position. In the process he became separated from the rest of Antony's fleet. This rapid turn of events bewildered the sailors in the center position. The commander of Octavian's center, **Lucius Arruntius**, didn't waste this opportunity. He moved in at once.

Even though Arruntius gained this tactical advantage, the battle continued all afternoon. Octavian's fleet would attack; Antony's would retreat. Then Antony's fleet would attack, and Octavian's would

The Battle of Actium

The Battle of Actium took place on the Ionian Sea in 31 BCE. Although Marc Antony had more ships than Octavian, the deciding factor was experience. Octavian's navy had the advantage here. Even with the help of Cleopatra's 60 ships, Antony couldn't defeat Octavian.

retreat. Cleopatra grew increasingly anxious. Worried that she would suffer great losses if the battle continued, she ordered her ships to leave the scene of the fighting and return home. Antony abandoned his fleet and followed her.

As the battle came to an end, Octavian's navy had killed 5,000 of Antony's sailors.[1] Only a quarter of Antony's ships had escaped after

CHAPTER 1

This painting of the Battle of Actium was completed in 1672 by Lorenzo A. Castro, centuries after the actual event took place. Although he wasn't there to witness the battle himself, Castro did an excellent job of capturing what historians say happened during the fight.

he deserted them. Octavian seized the others, along with the treasure they held. He had won the battle, but it would be another year before he would make his way to Egypt for his final confrontation with the pair.

The Quinquereme

At Actium, some of the largest ships involved in the fighting were the **quinqueremes**. Octavian used a quinquereme as the flagship of his navy in the battle. Antony had many of these long, narrow ships among his own fleet.

Quinqueremes were about 150 feet (45 meters) in length. Since quin- is the prefix for five, some people believed that meant five sets of oars on each side. It seems more likely, however, that there were two sets with three men on one oar and two on the other. Or there could have been three sets. The oars on two would have had two oarsmen, with one on the third. Besides the rowers, each quinquereme probably carried between 50 and 100 fighting men and a small number of sailors.

The vessels were made of heavy square timbers called wales. These timbers were secured to one another with long iron bolts. To make the ships even stronger, the bows of the quinqueremes were covered with bronze plates. The quinquereme's strong structure made it almost impossible for smaller vessels to ram it without breaking apart.

In one way, though, the quinquereme's size put it at a disadvantage. It was not as maneuverable as smaller ships.

A sculpture called Young Octavian (circa 1873) by Edmonia Lewis is on display in the Smithsonian American Art Museum. It is a copy of a sculpture in the Vatican galleries that was created in the late 18th or early 19th century.

CHAPTER 2
The Boy Known as Octavius

Augustus Caesar was born in Rome just before sunrise on the morning of September 23, 63 BCE.[1] He was given his father's name, **Gaius Octavius Thurinus**. He would be known by several different names during his lifetime, however. Most of his family and friends called him Octavius during his early years.

Octavius would never really know his father, who died when he was just four years old.[2] Octavius' mother, **Atia**, remarried a year later. His stepfather's name was Philippus. But Philippus wouldn't have a significant impact on his life. Atia was the niece of Julius Caesar, who would later become the most powerful man in Rome. It was this relationship that would affect Octavius's life the most.

Octavius wasn't a very healthy child. He limped on his left side and certainly didn't seem much like a future leader of Rome at this time. Still, Octavius didn't let his physical challenges hold him back. He was determined to learn and do all that he could.

CHAPTER 2

Octavius's grandmother Julia—Julius Caesar's sister—died when he was 12 years old. Already well-spoken, he took it upon himself to deliver the eulogy at her funeral. The handsome young man with curly blond hair and a pleasant voice impressed everyone in attendance.

As a teenager, Octavius was a bright and dedicated scholar. He studied literature and philosophy as well as law and government. He spent large amounts of time in Rome's courts, listening to lawyers argue cases.

Octavius had a strong talent for attracting people. His connection to Julius Caesar also increased his influence. Caesar had risen to power in Rome in 48 after winning a civil war. Other young men who wanted careers in politics hoped to earn a favor or two by supporting Caesar's nephew.

Atia worried that this family relationship could be dangerous. She knew that people saw Octavius as someone with influence on Rome's leader. It was how these people might try to deceive Octavius that worried her most.

Octavius and Caesar didn't spend much time together when Octavius was young. Their first known meeting came in 47 when Caesar returned to Rome from Egypt.[3] At this time Caesar decided to play a larger role in his nephew's life. He also arranged for Octavius to become a patrician.

Rome divided its citizens into two classes. The patricians were the higher class. Their noble status was handed down from one generation to the next. Caesar was already among this group, but Octavius was not. His mother was a patrician, but his father had been a plebian. This was the name given to everyone else in the city. And it was through a person's father that nobility was passed.

The label itself didn't change much for Octavius. His parents were quite wealthy by Roman standards. This act was simply Caesar's way of letting the world know that he considered Octavius as a part of his family. It was also an important step in preparing Octavius for a

The Boy Known as Octavius

This engraving depicts patricians during a banquet. A slave serves the men food and drink at a triclinium, a Roman dining table with couches on three sides.

future in government. Caesar went on to make Octavius the city prefect during the **Feriae Latinae**, one of Rome's major festivals. People came from all over to get a look at the attractive new prefect, the nephew of Julius Caesar.

Caesar later put his nephew in charge of the theatrical program of the triumphal celebrations. Octavius wanted to show his great-uncle what he could do. Even if the performance was long and the day was hot, he stayed until the very end. His dedication proved to be bad for his health, which was still weak. After a short time he fell gravely ill. When doctors told Caesar that his nephew might die, he ran barefoot though the streets to reach Octavius's bedside as quickly as possible.[4]

CHAPTER 2

This painting, "Cleopatra Before Caesar" by Jean-Leon Gerome, was finished in 1866. Sometimes referred to as "Cleopatra and Caesar," the piece shows her confronting Julius Caesar. After smuggling herself past the Roman guard, the Egyptian queen emerges from a rolled-up carpet. She stands with a single finger on a slave who crouches motionless at her side.

Caesar married three times during his lifetime. He also had a passionate love affair with Queen Cleopatra of Egypt. None of these relationships had given him a legitimate heir, however.

Without an heir, Caesar would have no one to carry on his name or to inherit his role as the leader of Rome. He thought that perhaps Octavius could take over when the time came. No one knew just how soon that day would come, though.

Learning Opportunities

Wealthy Roman families hired tutors to teach their children basic skills like reading and writing. Because most families could not afford to do this, many people who lived during this period could neither read nor write.

Not all poor families were uneducated, though. Parents passed whatever knowledge they had on to their young children. Fathers who could read and write passed these skills on to their sons. When possible, mothers taught their daughters to read and write, as well as how to spin and weave. Public schooling was available for boys, but it wasn't done in schools as we think of them today. Many schools of this time were simply the back rooms of shops where a teacher and a small number of students would gather.

In this era, education was considered more important for boys than for girls. Boys from well-to-do families would learn Greek and study literature. At the age of 17, patrician boys would go on to learn about philosophy. They would also practice their public speaking.  Young men who came from upper-class families, as Octavius did, were expected to enter politics.

This bust of Augustus Caesar, found in the Ara Pacis Museum in Rome, was modeled after a portrait of the ruler. The original piece of art is on display in the Musei Capitolini in Rome.

CHAPTER 3
Proving His Worth

When Octavius was 17, Caesar left for a campaign in Spain. He wanted his nephew to go with him, but ill health got in the way again. Instead, Octavius agreed to make the trip as soon as he recovered. He was eager to follow through on this promise.

Atia was worried about her son making the long and dangerous trip. He would be traveling in the winter and might encounter enemies along the way. At this point, however, Octavius was old enough to make his own decision. He chose a small group of servants to accompany him instead.

When Octavius finally reached Spain, Caesar had already completed what had been a victorious campaign. Octavius was happy with the outcome, but disappointed that he hadn't been able to prove his value on the battlefield. Nonetheless, Caesar was impressed with his nephew's enthusiasm and loyalty. Not everyone supported him so fully.

Both men were in need of some rest. It is said that Caesar suffered from extreme dizzy spells.

CHAPTER 3

Today we know that he probably had a condition called epilepsy. After spending some time with his great-uncle and further impressing him with his organizational and political skills, Octavius returned home shortly before he turned 18. He remained with his mother and stepfather until late 45.[1] Then his great-uncle sent him to **Apollonia**,

Proving His Worth

a city which is now part of the country of Albania. Octavius would spend the next four months there, completing his education and getting ready to join Caesar's army.

Caesar made sure that his nephew had every advantage. He even hired a highly-respected teacher named **Apollodorus of Pergamum**

The ruins of Apollonia are located about 80 miles outside the city of Fier in Albania. When Octavius traveled there, it was an important cultural center. An earthquake in the area during the third century CE marked the beginning of the city's decline.

CHAPTER 3

to be Octavius's tutor. While in Apollonia, Octavius studied literature in both Greek and Latin. He also studied a special style of public speaking called elocution.

In addition to his studies, Octavius trained with the cavalry. Because of his relation to Caesar, Octavius was already thought of as a high-status member of the group. He became friendly with many high-ranking officers. They listened eagerly when he spoke of his uncle's Spanish campaign.

Octavius was expecting Caesar to join him in Apollonia. The plan was for his great-uncle to lead the army in a battle against Parthia, located in modern-day Iran. Octavius looked forward to joining in the campaign. But he was heading to dinner with his companions one afternoon when a messenger arrived with a letter. It was written by his mother and contained devastating news. His great-uncle had been assassinated.

The messenger told Octavius what he knew of the event. He said that a large number of people had been involved in the plot to kill his great-uncle. The mother who had been so overprotective of her sickly son now had genuine reason to worry for his safety. Atia asked him to return home at once. She wrote, "You must show yourself a man now and consider what you ought to do, and implement your plans as fortune and opportunity allow."[2]

The Assassination of Julius Caesar

On the morning of March 15, 44 BCE, Julius Caesar's wife **Calpurnia** told him about a terrible dream she'd had during the previous night. She believed it was a sign that something terrible was going to happen that day and urged him to stay home. Caesar continued with his plans to meet with the Senate.

When Caesar arrived at the meeting hall, he took his usual chair. Normally Mark Antony would be seated beside him. On this morning, however, Antony was in another chamber with one of the men who were plotting against Caesar. No one knows for certain if he was part of the plan or if he had been led away purposely, since he was a trusted friend of Caesar.

Shortly after Caesar sat down, a large group of senators surrounded him. One grabbed his toga to keep him from getting up. Before Caesar realized what was happening, someone else had stabbed him from behind. He might have had a chance against a single attacker, but man after man came at him. When all was said and done, the group had inflicted a total of 23 wounds on his body.[3]

The Death of Julius Caesar by Vincenzo Camuccini (1798)

Nineteenth century German artist Heinrich Spiess shows Antony's reaction to Caesar's death in his print, "Julius Caesar, Mark Antony's Funeral Oration Over the Corpse of Caesar."

CHAPTER 4
Caesar's Will

Antony appeared to be devastated by the loss of his friend, Julius Caesar. He even gave the eulogy at his funeral. He seemed so grief-stricken that the people in attendance reacted with great passion. They banded together and drove the assassins out of the city.

Caesar's will was read a few days later. Antony thought that he would surely be named the ruler's chief heir. He was in for a big surprise. Caesar had updated the document shortly after the Spanish campaign with his wish to adopt Octavius. He also named his great-nephew his successor—and the recipient of the bulk of his enormous fortune.

Caesar remembered all the citizens of Rome in his will. The dictator had owned beautiful gardens along the Tiber River. This land would now be used as a public park. He also left money to all Roman citizens. Each person was to receive 300 sesterces.[1]

Atia and Philippus both wanted Octavius to turn down the inheritance. They thought that a life in Roman politics would be a dangerous one.

CHAPTER 4

They urged Octavius to return home and to keep his own name. He knew they had made some valid points. Still, Octavius felt compelled to take Ceasar's name. He quickly vowed to avenge his adoptive father's death and take his rightful place as the ruler of Rome.

It would be a number of months before the adoption was made official. This didn't stop Octavius from using his new name: Gaius Julius Caesar Octavianus. Today most historians refer to him as Octavian when speaking of this period of his life. It also didn't stop Caesar's army from welcoming Octavian as their new leader. The men clearly saw him as Caesar's son.

Although Antony was shut out of Caesar's will, he still remained an important member of the Senate. He planned to keep as much political power as possible. Before Octavian's adoption would become final, Antony was placed in charge of Caesar's financial resources. Many people suspected that he had stolen from these riches. Before Caesar's death, Antony was forty million sesterces in debt. Now his financial problems were gone with no explanation of how or why.

Octavian asked Antony for the money that Caesar had left his people. He wanted to give the citizens their rightful inheritance. Antony refused, claiming that he had found the state treasury empty following Caesar's death. He also pointed out that the adoption was not yet final, a fact with which Octavian could not argue. Antony did his best in the upcoming months to delay the adoption as long as possible. In the meantime, though, Octavian saw it as his duty to follow through on Caesar's promise to the people.

He put all of Caesar's properties up for sale and paid the people their inheritance out of his own pocket. He had to borrow money from his mother, stepfather, and two cousins to make this happen. The act made him even more popular with the people of Rome. Still, it seemed that he wasn't going to be able to accomplish much with Antony as an enemy.

Soon, though, the two men realized that they could accomplish more as allies. In 43 they decided to join forces with **Marcus Lepidus**,

Caesar's Will

one of Caesar's former generals, and formed a group of three rulers called a triumvirate.[2]

They needed money. They could not command an army without paying the soldiers. To solve this problem, they came up with a harsh plan. They decided to punish every person involved in the assassination plot against Caesar with death. They made a list of 300 senators and 2,000 members of Rome's upper middle class.[3] The triumvirs—Octavian, Antony, and Lepidus—knew that each person on the list owned large amounts of property that would fetch equally large amounts of money.

W.H. Weston depicts Brutus and his companions following the Battle of Philippi in this illustration from his book, *Plutarch's Lives for Boys and Girls*.

Some of the men they targeted were indeed involved in the plot to kill Caesar. Most, though, had had nothing to do with the assassination. Many of the accused decided to flee. These men surrendered their property, but they kept their lives. The ones who did not leave were killed.

The plan raised enough money for the triumvirate to challenge the armies of Caesar's two main assassins, Marcus Brutus and **Cassius**. The two men had fled Rome following the murder. In 42, the

CHAPTER 4

Brutus chose to die by falling on his own sword instead of being captured and killed by his enemies. He, like many men of this era, saw this type of act as one of courage and honor. It was also a way of denying one's enemy the accomplishment.

triumvirate led an army that traveled to Greece to track down the former senators.[4] Octavian was finally going to avenge Caesar's death.

The respective armies clashed at the Greek town of Philippi. As Antony gained some ground on Cassius's men, Brutus broke into Octavian's camp. Cassius, though, was unaware of his fellow assassin's success. Thinking he was going to be captured, Cassius ordered a freedman to kill him. Brutus hung on to his position for a fortnight, but the triumvirate eventually gained the upper hand. Like his ally, Brutus would not allow himself to be killed by his enemies.

Instead he fell on his own sword, ending his life.

Remembering the Romans

Flip through your calendar, and you will find three examples of how Augustus Caesar and his famous great-uncle left a permanent mark on the world. When Julius Caesar rose to power, the first month of the year was March. Wanting a month to be named after him, Caesar changed the name of fifth month, then called Quintilius, to Julius. It would later become known as July.

Like Julius Caesar, Augustus wanted a month named for him. He changed the name of the sixth month, Sextilius, to Augustus. Of course, we now call it August.

Augustus also had a hand in making February the shortest month of the year. Donald Phillips of the Polytechnic Institute of New York University told the story of how February ended up with fewer days than all the other months. When Augustus came into power, August had 30 days. Phillips explained that Augustus was upset that July had 31 days while "his" month had only 30. It seems that Augustus thought a month with fewer days than his great-uncle's was somehow less of an honor. "So he pulls a day from February and adds it to August so he'll have as many days as Julius,"[5] Phillips explained.

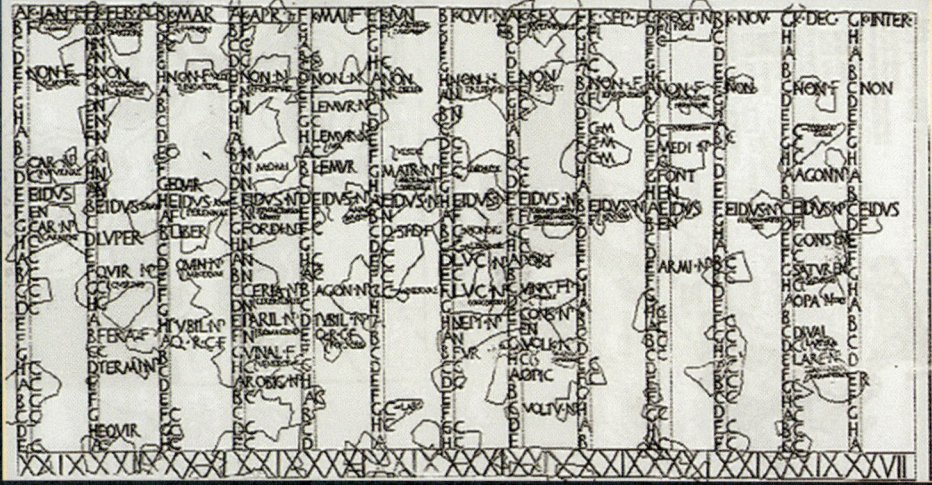

Image of a fresco of a calendar from before the time of Julius Caesar

This marble statue of Augustus as Pontifex Maximus was created from two types of marble. The head and arms were formed from Greek marble, and the body was sculpted from Italian marble. The statue was completed during the last decade of the first century CE.

CHAPTER 5
The "Roman Peace"

Octavian and his fellow triumvirs agreed to divide up the Roman territories. Antony would rule the east. Octavian would control Gaul (modern-day France), Spain, and Italy (including Rome itself). Lepidus had North Africa. This arrangement worked for a few years, but Octavian forced Lepidus to retire in 36. The old rivalry between Octavian and Antony began again.

In 40, Antony had married Octavian's younger sister, Octavia.[1] Octavian arranged the marriage as a way to make an ally of Antony. It did not work. The couple divorced eight years later, because Antony had fallen in love with Cleopatra.[2] Marrying a foreigner was against Roman law. Nonetheless, Antony chose to make the queen his new wife. The Roman people were not happy about this turn of events, and Octavian was downright furious.

Antony responded by trying to convince the world that Octavian had no legal right to Caesar's name. The year after Cleopatra had met Julius Caesar, she gave birth to a son named Caesarion.

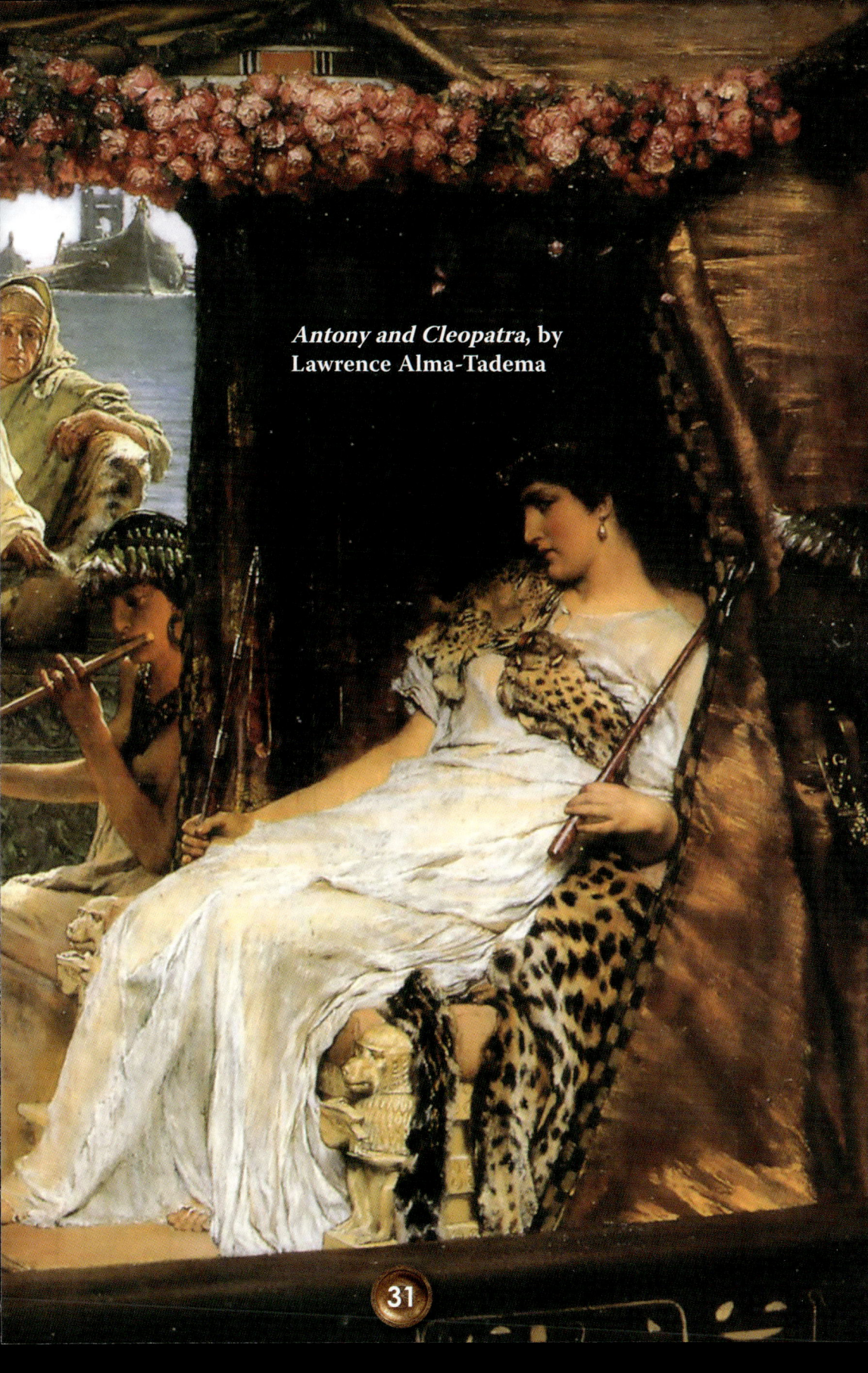
Antony and Cleopatra, by Lawrence Alma-Tadema

CHAPTER 5

This carving depicts Queen Cleopatra with her son, Caesarion. It is located at the Temple of Dendera in Egypt.

The "Roman Peace"

Antony claimed that the boy was Caesar's son, the rightful heir to his name and his empire.

It seemed that the only thing greater than Antony's hatred for Octavian was his love for Cleopatra. He left Rome to live in Egypt with the queen. Octavian knew that it was time to make a big move. He declared war in 31 and emerged victorius at Actium.[3]

A year later, Octavian invaded Egypt. When his army captured the capital city of Alexandria, Egypt became part of the Roman Empire. Antony and Cleopatra committed suicide. Octavian had Caesarion executed. It was time for the Roman world to move on with Octavian as its leader.

Pompeo Girolamo Batoni's painting "The Death of Marc Anthony" shows Antony dying after he had stabbed himself with his own sword.

CHAPTER 5

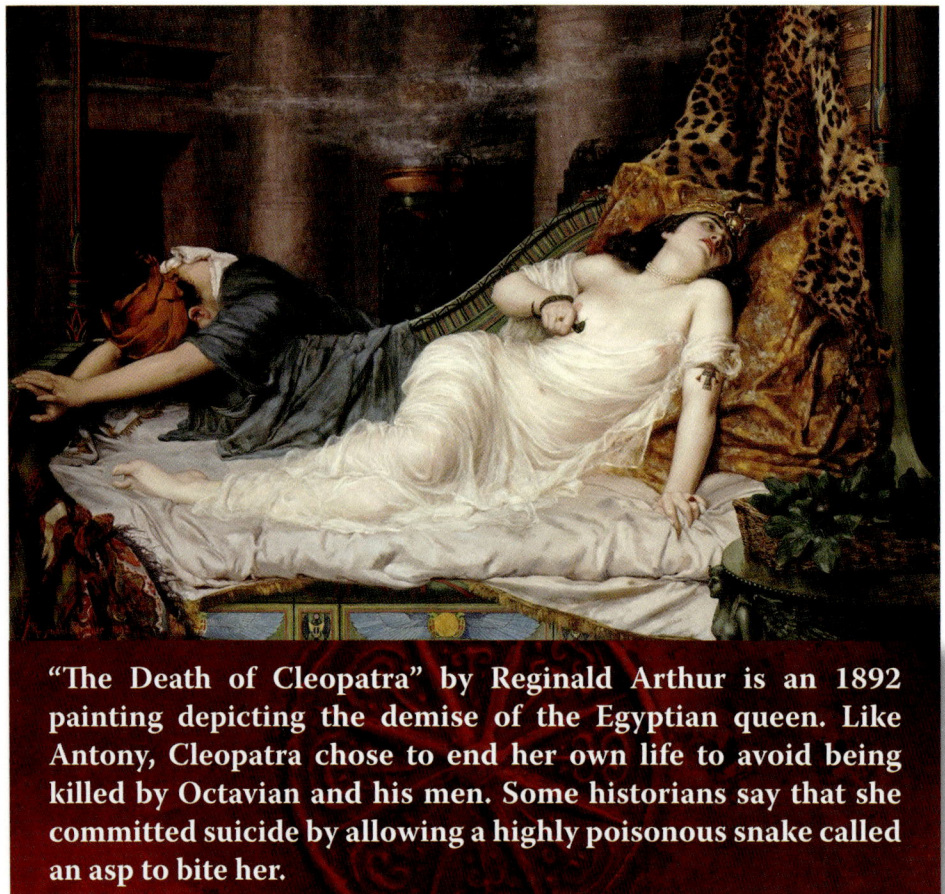

"The Death of Cleopatra" by Reginald Arthur is an 1892 painting depicting the demise of the Egyptian queen. Like Antony, Cleopatra chose to end her own life to avoid being killed by Octavian and his men. Some historians say that she committed suicide by allowing a highly poisonous snake called an asp to bite her.

Although Rome had been a republic for centuries, Octavian thought that Rome needed to be ruled by one man. Still, he knew that the Romans didn't like feeling like they had no say in their government. A talented speaker, he told the people that he wanted to return to the old ways of the republic. His plan, as he explained it to them, was to keep Rome's traditions alive while moving it into a bright future.

After decades of war, the people were eager for peace. Many people saw Augustus (the name by which he was now known) as the person who would make that peace possible. He took excellent care of the Romans, creating a safer and more pleasant place to live. He

The "Roman Peace"

made sure that the people had plenty of food. He spent large amounts of money building and repairing aqueducts to assure everyone a dependable source of clean water. He built a network of roads that made traveling easier. He created a police force and fire department to keep the people safe. He also filled Rome with numerous temples and monuments that created a happy and wealthy image for the city. He made religious traditions and festivals an important part of life in Rome once again. These efforts strengthened the people's positive image of him.

Augustus paid his soldiers very well. He offered them bonuses following large battles that took the men far away from home. Clearly he saw the expense as a way to earn their loyalty. And loyal was exactly what they were. Instead of just swearing an oath to the empire, Roman soldiers of this time pledged their devotion to Augustus himself as well.

He always made a point of appearing humble. He made a good show of making it seem like he didn't want too much power. He asked the Senate to limit his power to only a certain number of years. In 27, he even offered to give up his power altogether. His apparent willingness to step down caused the Senate to see him as a very fair man who could be trusted with more power, not less.

Augustus used this power to expand the Roman Empire in every direction. After bringing Egypt under the empire's control, he continued expanding farther into Africa. He also seized land along the eastern coast of the Adriatic Sea. He expanded the empire into Germany and finished what his great-uncle had begun by completing the conquest of Spain.

Although wars persisted in these outlying areas, Rome itself remained remarkably peaceful during Augustus's reign. He was a talented diplomat, creating peace with other empires such as the Parthians to the east. Perhaps what is most remarkable, though, is that peace lasted for more than two centuries. The era is now known as the *Pax Romana*, meaning the "Roman Peace."

CHAPTER 5

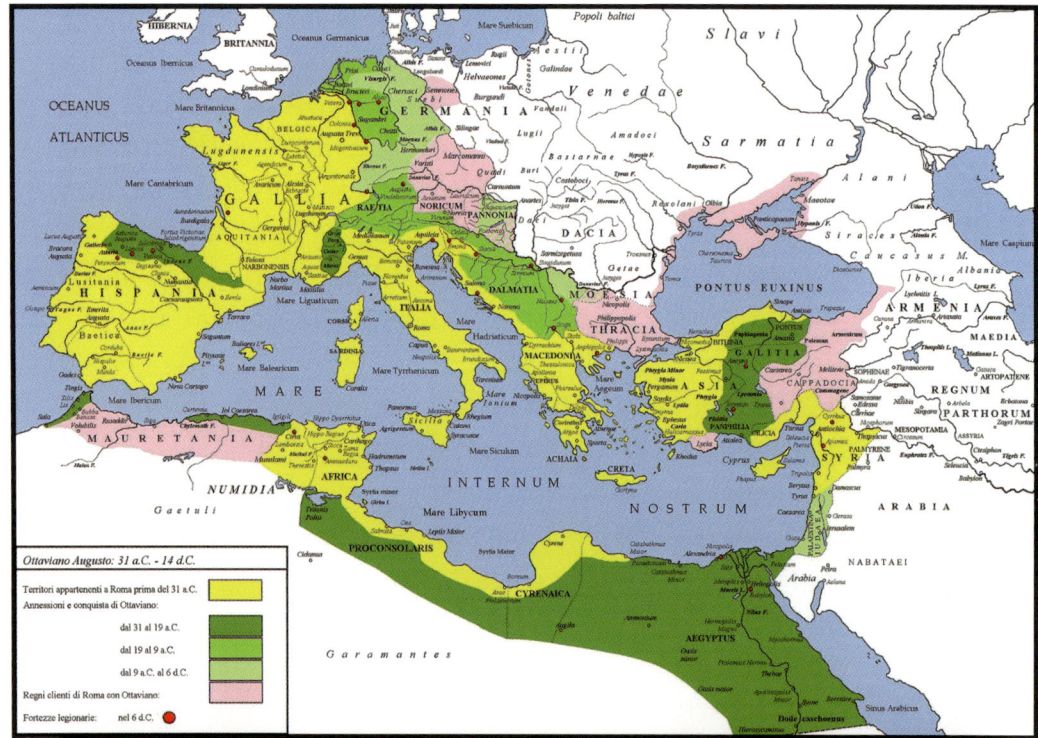

The Roman Empire expanded greatly under Augustus's reign. He completed the work that his great-uncle had begun, bringing Egypt, Germany, and Spain under Roman rule. His rule began a lengthy period of peace for the Roman people.

Augustus remained a revered figure in all of Rome's provinces. He made sure to earn this reverence through fair treatment. He instructed governors in these outlying areas to respect the customs of the native people. He also made a point of conducting a census regularly.[4] This step helped ensure that the tax system was fair. With every person counted, it was harder to avoid paying taxes to the Roman government.

Augustus encouraged the people of Rome to marry and have children. He believed that marriage should be a lifelong commitment, so he created laws that made divorce difficult. He wanted to build a

The "Roman Peace"

populous empire. He knew that marriage and family were the keys to making that happen.

Though he was twice divorced himself, Augustus did have a long and happy marriage with his third wife **Livia Drusilla**. The pair never had a child together, however. He had had a daughter with his second wife, but he could not leave his empire to a female child. Perhaps more than any other Roman, Augustus needed a son.

He adopted his sister's son, Marcellus, and planned to pass his empire on to him. Augustus ended up outliving the boy, however. He then adopted his two grandsons, but neither

Livia Drusilla statue located in the National Archaeological Museum of Spain in Madrid

This bust of Augustus's stepson and future emperor Tiberius was sculpted from a portrait. The painting from which it was modeled is found in the Ny Calrsberg Glyptotek in Copenhagen, Denmark.

of them lived long enough to claim their inheritance. Finally he decided to make his stepson Tiberius his heir.

Augustus Caesar lived a surprisingly long life as Rome's first emperor. When he died in 14 CE, the Roman Senate declared him a god. The boy who spent so much of his childhood in sickness went down in history as one of the most powerful men of all time.

The Mausoleum of Augustus

One of the first monuments that Augustus built during his time as emperor was a mausoleum for himself and his family. The enormous round tomb was located in the center of Rome. It was regarded as one of the most magnificent structures in Rome at the time. Nearly 300 feet (90 meters) in diameter and standing 150 feet (45 meters) high, the impressive monument was a symbol of the emperor's power and wealth.[4] Even more than that, though, it told the people that his reign would be a very important part of Roman history. From the very beginning, he was letting his people know that he would be remembered long after his death.

A bronze statue of Augustus was placed at the monument's highest point. Also, Augustus requested that two tablets be placed at the tomb's entrance. On them were inscribed his **Res Gestae**, a list of his most important accomplishments as head of the Roman Empire. Before the tomb served as Augustus's final resting place, he would open its doors for several of his relatives including his sister, nephew, and both his grandsons.

Mausoleum of Augustus in Rome

CHRONOLOGY

Dates BCE

63	Augustus Caesar is born as Gaius Octavius.
59	Octavius's father dies.
51	Julia, Octavius's grandmother, dies and he delivers the eulogy.
46	Octavius falls ill; is unable to go with Julius Caesar on his Spanish campaign.
45	Octavius travels to Spain to join his uncle, then goes to Apollonia to prepare for a campaign against Parthia.
44	Julius Caesar is assassinated; Octavius is named his heir and takes on name of Octavian.
43	Octavian, Antony, and Ledipus form the triumvirate; Octavian marries Clodia, Antony's step-daughter.
42	Octavian and Antony defeat Brutus and Cassius at the Battle of Philippi.
40	Antony marries Octavia, Octavian's sister; Octavian divorces Clodia and marries Scribonia.
39	Julia, Octavian's daughter, is born; Octavian divorces Scribonia.
38	Octavian marries Livia Drusilla.
32	Antony divorces Octavia.
31	Octavian defeats Antony and Cleopatra at Actium.
30	Antony and Cleopatra commit suicide, Octavian has Caesarion executed.
27	The Roman Empire is established and the Senate confers the name Augustus Caesar on Octavian.
26	Augustus leads a campaign in Spain.
22-19	Augustus tours the East, including Athens, Ephesus, and Syria.
17	Augustus adopts his grandsons, Gaius and Lucius, as his heirs.
16-13	Augustus tours Gaul and Spain.
12	Augustus meets with Herod the Great in Aquileia.
6	Augustus falls ill in Rome, but recovers.

CHRONOLOGY

Dates CE
2   Augustus's grandson Lucius dies.
4   Augustus's grandson Gaius dies; Augustus adopts his stepson, Tiberius, as his heir.
14   Augustus dies.

Bust of Augustus wearing the Civic Crown. This sculpture is in the Glyptothek Museum in Munich, Germany

TIMELINE

Dates BCE

133	Tiberius Gracchus is killed after suggesting that public lands be given to the peasants of Rome.
121	Gaius, Tiberius's brother, is killed when more reforms are proposed.
107	Gaius Marius is elected consul.
100	Julius Caesar is born.
91-89	Rome battles several former allies in the Social War.
88	Lucius Cornelius Sulla becomes dictator of Rome.
73-71	Spartacus leads slave revolt; he is killed by Marcus Crassus.
70	Pompey and Crassus become consuls.
60	Julius Caesar becomes consul.
48	Julius Caesar defeats Pompey and becomes the most powerful man in Rome.

Dates CE

14	Tiberius becomes emperor of Rome.
37	Tiberius dies and is succeeded by Caligula.
41	Caligula is assassinated; Claudius succeeds him.
54	Nero becomes emperor after the death of Claudius.
64	The Great Fire of Rome destroys much of the city.
68	Nero commits suicide; he is the last emperor related to Julius Caesar.
79	Mt. Vesuvius erupts, burying Pompeii and surrounding cities under ash.

CHAPTER NOTES

Chapter 1—The Battle of Actium
1. "Battle of Actium in 31 B.C. Changed the World." *Hindustan Times*, March 31, 2008.
2. Richard A. Gabriel, "Masters of the Mediterranean." *Military History*, December 2007.

Chapter 2—The Boy Known as Octavius
1. Richard A. Gabriel, *Great Captains of Antiquity* (Santa Barbara, California: Praeger, 2000), p. 184.
2. Episode 1: Order from Chaos – The Roman Empire in the First Century. Public Broadcasting System. http://www.pbs.org/empires/romans/series/transcript1.html
3. Anthony Everitt, *Augustus: The Life of Rome's First Emperor* (New York: Random House, 2006), p. 35.
4. Ibid., p. 43.

Chapter 3—Proving His Worth
1. Anthony Everitt, *Augustus: The Life of Rome's First Emperor* (New York: Random House, 2006), p. 49.
2. Ibid., p. 52.
3. Ibid., p. 55.

Chapter 4—Caesar's Will
1. Anthony Everitt, *Augustus: The Life of Rome's First Emperor* (New York: Random House, 2006), p. 56.
2. "Mark Antony," History.com. http://www.history.com/topics/mark-antony
3. Samuel Griswold Goodrich, *Ancient History: From the Creation to the Fall of Rome, A.D. 476* (Charleston, South Carolina: Nabu Press, 2011), p. 501.
4. John Buchan, *Augustus* (Boston, Massachusetts: Houghton Mifflin, 1937), p. 62.
5. Marilyn Goldstein, "Make March of Time Up-Tempo." *Newsday* (Nassau and Suffolk Edition), March 8, 1993.

Chapter 5—The "Roman Peace"
1. Anthony Everitt, *Augustus: The Life of Rome's First Emperor* (New York: Random House, 2006), p. 112.
2. Ibid., p. 174.
3. "The Battle of Actium," This Day in History: September 2. http://www.history.com/this-day-in-history/the-battle-of-actium4. Everitt, *Augustus*, p. 231.

FURTHER READING

Books

Foster, Genevieve. *Augustus Caesar's World: A Story of Ideas and Events from B.C. 44 to 14 A.D.* San Luis Obispo, California: Beautiful Feet Books, 1996.

James, Simon. *Anicent Rome.* New York: DK Eyewitness Books, 2008.

MacDonald, Fiona. *100 Facts on Ancient Rome.* Essex, United Kingdom: Miles Kelly Publishing, 2010.

Whiting, Jim. *The Life and Times of Augustus Caesar.* Hockessin, Delaware: Mitchell Lane Publishers, 2005.

Works Consulted

"The Battle of Actium," This Day in History: September 2. http://www.history.com/this-day-in-history/the-battle-of-actium

Buchan, John. *Augustus.* Boston, Massachusetts, Houghton Mifflin Company, 1937.

Earl, Donald. *The Age of Augustus.* New York: Crown Publishers, 1968.

Everitt, Anthony. *Augustus: The Life of Rome's First Emperor.* New York: Random House, 2006.

Gabriel, Richard A. "Masters of the Mediterranean." *Military History*, December 2007.

"Octavian/Augustus," Ancient Worlds: The Roman World. http://www.ancientworlds.net/aw/Article/826992

Porter, Barry. "Rome's Fate in the Balance." *Military History*, August 1997.

Wells, Peter S. *The Battle That Stopped Rome.* New York, New York: W.W. Norton & Company, 2003.

FURTHER READING

On the Internet

BBC History: Augustus Caesar
http://www.bbc.co.uk/history/historic_figures/augustus.shtml

History of Augustus Caesar
http://www.historyworld.net/wrldhis/plaintexthistories.asp?historyid=aa09

Augustus, History Channel
http://www.history.com/topics/emperor-augustus

The Roman Empire in the First Century: Augustus Caesar
http://www.pbs.org/empires/romans/empire/augustus.html

Aureus of Octavian, circa 30 BCE. This golden coin is displayed at the British Museum in London, England.

PHONETIC PRONUNCIATIONS

Actium (AK-tee-uhm)
Apollodorus of Pergamum (ah-pawl-uh-DOR-uhs)
Atia (ah-TEE-uh)
Augustus Caesar (ah-GUS-tuhs SEE-zer)
Cassius (KASS-ee-uhs)
Cleopatra (klee-oh-PAH-truh)
Feriae Latinae (FAYHR-ee-ay LAH-tin-ay)
Gaius Octavius Thurinus (GUY-uhs ok-TAV-ee-uhs THUR-i-nuhs)
Livia Drusilla (LIV-ee-uh dru-SIL-uh)
Lucius Policola (LOO-see-uhs pol-i-KOH-luh)
Lucius Arruntius (LOO-see-uhs uh-RUN-tee-uhs)
Marcus Agrippa (MAR-kuhs ah-GRIP-uh)
Marcus Lepidus (MAR-kuhs LEP-i-duhs)
Octavian (ok-TAV-ee-uhn)
Quinquereme (KWIN-kwe-reem)
Res Gestae (REZ jes-TAY)

Bronze statue of Emperor Augustus Caesar on Via Dei Fori Imperiali, Rome, Italy

GLOSSARY

ally (AL-Iye)—A person, group, or nation associated with another for a common purpose.

aqueduct (AW-kwuh-duhkt)—An artificial channel that carries water over a long distance.

assassinate (uh-SA-suh-nate)—To kill an important person.

campaign (kam-PAYN)—Military operations for a specific objective.

cavalry (KA-vuhl-ree)—A military group made up of soldiers on horseback.

census (SEN-suss)—The registration of citizens and their property, often for tax purposes.

consul (KOHN-suhl)—One of two chief magistrates of the ancient Roman Republic.

diplomat (DIP-loh-mat)—A person who maintains political, economic, and social relations with another country on behalf of his own country.

epilepsy (EH-puh-lep-see)—A disorder of the nervous system characterized by seizures.

eulogy (YOO-luh-jee)—A speech given in honor of a deceased person.

fortnight (FOHRT-nite)—A period of 14 days.

freedman (FREED-man)—A man who has been freed from slavery.

mausoleum (maw-suh-LEE-uhm)—A large stone building with tombs for one or more people.

prefect (PREE-fekt)—A person nominated as chief magistrate of an event in ancient Rome.

province (PRAW-vinss)—Administrative division of a country or an empire.

PHOTO CREDITS: Cover, pp. 1, 14—Jean-Léon Gérôme; pp. 4, 46—Photos.com; pp. 7—Lencer/Leo—cc-by-sa-3.0; p. 8—Lorenzo A. Castro; p. 10—Edmonia Lewis; p. 13—Prisma/UIG/Getty Images; pp. 16, 18–19, 38—B. Marvis; p. 21—Vincenzo Camuccini; p. 22—Heinrich Spiess; pp. 25, 26, 27—Library of Congress; p. 28—Ryan Freisling/PD-SELF; pp. 30–31—Lawrence Alma-Tadema; p. 32—Rowan; p. 33—Pompeo Girolamo Batoni; p. 34—Reginald Arthur; p. 36—Cristiano64/cc-by-sa-3.0; p. 37—Zaqarbal/National Archaeological Museum of Spain; p. 39—ryarwood/cc-by-sa-2.0; p. 41—Palace Bevilacqua, Verona; p. 45—PHGCOM/British Museum. Every effort has been made to locate all copyright holders of materials used in this book. Any errors or omissions will be corrected in future editions of the book.

INDEX

adoption   23–24, 37

Apollodorus of Pergamum   19–20

Apollonia   18–20

Antony, Mark   5–7, 9, 21, 22, 23–26, 29, 30–31, 33, 34

Atia   11–12, 17, 20, 23

assassination   5, 20–21, 25

aqueduct   35

August   27

Brutus, Marcus Junius   25-26

Caesar, Julia (grandmother)   12

Caesar, Julius   5, 11, 12–14, 21, 22, 23–24, 27, 29

Caesarion   29, 32, 33

Calpurnia   21

Cassius (Cassius Longinus)   25–26

cavalry   20

Cleopatra   5–7, 14, 29, 30–31, 32, 33, 34

census   36

education   15, 19

Egypt   5–6, 8, 12, 14, 32, 33, 35, 36

epilepsy   12, 18, 23

eulogy   12, 22–23

Gaul (France)   29

health   11, 13, 17

July   27

Lepidus, Marcus Aemilius   24–25, 29

Livia Drusilla   37

Marcellus   37

Mausoleum of Augustus   39

monuments   35, 39

patricians   12–13, 15

Philippi, Battle of   25–26

Philippus   11, 23

plebians   12

republic   34

Roman Empire   5–6, 33, 35, 36, 39

Senate   21, 24, 35, 38

Spain   17, 29, 35, 36

Thurinus, Gaius Octavius (father)   11

Thurinus, Gaius Octavius (son)   11

Tiberius   38

triumvir   25–26, 29